Hydroponic Tomatoes

By Heather Hammonds

Illustrations by Sharyn Madder

Contents

Juicy and Delicious

Zac and Dad walked towards the car park
carrying their bags of groceries.
"Let's buy some tomatoes
from the hydroponic tomato farm
on the way home," said Dad.
"Grandma is coming to lunch today.
She likes tomatoes in a salad."

“Oh, no!” groaned Zac.
“Dad, you know I don’t like tomatoes.
Grandma always tells me to eat them.
She says they are good for me.”

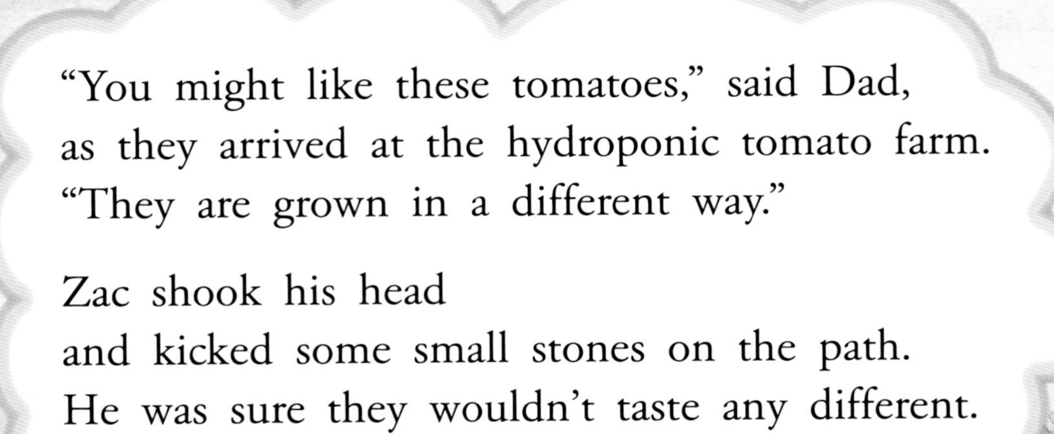

"You might like these tomatoes," said Dad,
as they arrived at the hydroponic tomato farm.
"They are grown in a different way."

Zac shook his head
and kicked some small stones on the path.
He was sure they wouldn't taste any different.

There were lots of greenhouses at the farm.
A farmer took Zac and his dad
into the biggest greenhouse.

The farmer picked a juicy tomato
and gave it to Zac.

Zac felt his stomach go tight,
but he didn't want to upset the farmer
by not eating the tomato.

Zac closed his eyes
and took a big bite of the tomato.
To his amazement it was delicious.

"I like **these** tomatoes," said Zac.
"Won't Grandma be surprised
when she comes to lunch
and sees me eating them!"

Tasty Hydroponic Tomatoes

We believe that everyone
should eat hydroponic tomatoes.

First, tomatoes are very good for us.
They have lots of vitamins in them,
to help keep us healthy and strong.

Second, hydroponic tomatoes are picked
when they are ripe and juicy,
so they taste delicious.

Third, hydroponic tomatoes grow in greenhouses,
so they look much better
than tomatoes that grow in gardens.

Hydroponic tomatoes have smooth, shiny, red skins.
They don't have marks on them,
made by birds, the wind or the rain.

Tasty
Hydroponic Tomatoes

We believe that everyone
should eat hydroponic tomatoes.

First, tomatoes are very good for us.
They lots of vitamins in them,
keep us healthy and

Second,
so they taste delicious.

Third, hydroponic tomatoes grow in greenhouses,
so they look much better
than tomatoes that grow in gardens.

Hydroponic tomatoes have smooth, shiny, red skins.
They don't have marks on them,
made by birds, the wind, or the rain.

Fourth, hydroponic tomato farmers
tomato plants.
This helps them grow
the biggest, tastiest tomatoes.

Hydroponic tomatoes grow
almost all year round.
They are delivered fresh to markets,
greengrocers and supermarkets every day.

Finally, hydroponic tomatoes are delicious
in sandwiches and salads.
You can even eat them on their own!

We think you should buy
some hydroponic tomatoes
and see how good they taste.

Fourth, hydroponic tomato farmers
put special plant food
in the water of the tomato plants.
This helps them grow
the biggest, tastiest tomatoes.

Hydroponic tomatoes grow
almost all year round.
They are delivered fresh to markets,
greengrocers and supermarkets every day.

Finally, hydroponic tomatoes are delicious
in sandwiches and salads.
You can even eat them on their own!

We think you should buy
some hydroponic tomatoes
and see how good they taste.

Tasty

Hydroponic Tomatoes

We believe that everyone
should eat hydroponic tomatoes.

First, tomatoes are very good for us.
They have lots of vitamins in them,
to help keep us healthy and strong.

Second, hydroponic tomatoes are picked
when they are ripe and juicy,
so they taste delicious.

Third, hydroponic tomatoes grow in greenhouses,
so they look much better
than tomatoes that grow in gardens.

Hydroponic tomatoes have smooth, shiny, red skins.
They don't have marks on them,
made by birds, the wind, or the rain.

Fourth, hydroponic tomato farmers
put special plant food
in the water of the tomato plants.
This helps them grow
the biggest, tastiest tomatoes.

Hydroponic tomatoes grow
almost all year round.
They are delivered fresh to marke
greengrocers and supermarkets

Finally, hydroponic tomatoes are delicious
in sandwiches and salads.
You can even eat them on their own!

We think you should buy
some hydroponic tomatoes
and see how good they taste.